Good Housekeeping

Simple
and
Stunning
Flowers

Good Housekeeping

Simple and Stunning Flowers

Mary Jane Vaughan

special photography by Marie-Louise Avery

EBURY PRESS
LONDON

First published in 1998

3 5 7 9 10 8 6 4 2

Text © Ebury Press 1998
Photographs © Ebury Press and/or the National Magazine Company 1998

All rights reserved. No part of this publication may be reproduced, stored in a retrieval system, or transmitted in any form
or by any means, electronic, mechanical, photocopying or otherwise without the prior permission of the copyright owners.

The expression GOOD HOUSEKEEPING as used in the title of the book is the trade mark of the National Magazine
Company Limited and the Hearst Corporation, registered in the United Kingdom and USA, and other principal courntries
of the world and is the absolute property of the National Magazine Company Limited and the Hearst Corporation. The use
of this trade mark other than with the express permission of the National Magazine Company Limited or the Hearst
Corporation is strictly prohibited.

First published in the United Kingdom in 1998 by Ebury Press
Random House, 20 Vauxhall Bridge Road, London SW1V 2SA

Random House Australia (Pty) Limited
20 Alfred Street, Milsons Point, Sydney,
New South Wales 2061, Australia

Random House New Zealand Limited
18 Poland Road, Glenfield, Auckland 10, New Zealand

Random House South Africa (Pty) Limited
Endulini, 5a Jubilee Road, Parktown 2193, South Africa

Random House UK Limited Reg. No. 954009

A CIP catalogue record for this book is available from the British Library.

ISBN 0 09 185352 4

Project editor Emma Callery
Stylist for special photography Helen Trent
Designed by Christine Wood

Colour reproduction by Colourpath
Printed and bound in Singapore by Tien Wah Press

The Good Housekeeping Institute

The Good Housekeeping Institute was created in 1924 to provide readers of *Good Housekeeping*
magazine with expert consumer advice and delicious, classic and contemporary easy-to-follow recipes.
These ideals still hold true today. The Institute team are all experienced cooks, home economists and
consumer researchers. They test the latest products in purpose-built, modern kitchens, where every
recipe published in the magazine and its range of best-selling cookery books is developed and rigorously
tested so that you can cook any GH recipe with confidence. When any new ingredient appears on
supermarket shelves, you can be sure that GH has tried and tasted it way ahead and interpreted a food
trend into a workable, stylish recipe.

Television crews and radio broadcast units are regular visitors to the renowned Institute kitchens, which
have become a popular location for leading food and consumer programmes.

Good Housekeeping magazine's authority and experience go well beyond the kitchen and cooking.
The Institute can also tell you the best buys in anything from wine to computers and luxury lingerie. The
Good Housekeeping Institute is synonymous with quality and impartial advice, offering good value for the
consumer. You can trust the authority of *Good Housekeeping*'s word on health, careers, holidays, family
matters and fashion and beauty. Over two million people buy it, read it and live by it.

Contents

Introduction	6		
Basic Techniques	8	Winter	64
Spring	10	Special Occasions	82
Summer	30	Seasonal Colour Directory	100
Autumn	46	Index	104

Introduction

In one way or another, I have been involved with flowers for most of my life. I grew up in Colombia with a flower growing family and I now have two flower shops in London, so I am literally surrounded by flowers all the time.

It always amazes me how I still gasp with delight on opening a box of sweet peas, receiving a tray of gardenias, or working with a new variety of a rose or a tulip. And I don't think it is only me who feels like this. I know of nobody who is oblivious to the beauty, simplicity and freshness of flowers.

So when I put together this book, I had lots of fun as I was able to arrange flowers as they look best: simply. I could allow the flowers to speak for themselves. This is something that I have always striven for in my designs, preferring to use simple, everyday blooms, rather than seeking out more exotic ones that can be difficult to get hold of. By grouping them as single varieties, selecting a few colours that work together especially well, combining flowers with fruits and perhaps a few vegetables, or choosing striking containers, I find that I am able to do so much with so little. The wonderful photographs on these pages show you just what can be achieved. I hope that they will inspire you to arrange flowers simply – and stunningly – in your home.

Basic techniques

The simplest of ideas are the ones that generally work best. So, for this book, we have chosen designs that are easy to put together, and also look simple – and, of course, stunning. There is no wiring or other complicated techniques to cope with. In fact, there are really no techniques at all, except for a few hints that will make your designs look better for longer.

Buying flowers

No matter how cheap the flowers may seem, it is never a good deal to buy open flowers. Instead, buy flowers when they are in bud and beginning to open. Apart from this, look for any blemishes or marks on the leaves as having none is always a good sign of good health in flowers. When you take the flowers home, trim the stems, taking off about 1 cm (½ in), and place the flowers in cold water with some flower food (see below). Keep them in a well-aired, cool place until you want to use them for an arrangement.

Keeping flowers fresh for longer

Cut flowers depend on fresh water to live so it is important to keep the flow of water unobstructed up the stem. To do this, do not crush the end of the stems as this may only obstruct the flow of water. Instead, cut the stems at an angle, using a sharp knife; the angle will expose more area to the water, and the sharpness of the knife will ensure that there is no stem damage. Also remove any leaves that would otherwise be underwater, as they may rot.

Keep the water in your container clean at all times. If the water is not clean, bacteria will form that can prevent the passage of water up to the flower – as well as making the water cloudy and smelly!

To further extend the life of cut flowers, use some flower food or preservative in the water. This can be home-made or bought commercially. Once a flower has been cut, the process of photosynthesis, through which a plant obtains most of its energy from the sun and soil, will have been interrupted. But a cut flower continues to need energy to open up and develop to its full potential, and so it is necessary to provide an alternative supply of energy. Cut flower food provides this. It also contains acidifiers to aid water intake and provides anti-bacterial agents. These keep the water free from bacteria and other micro-organisms that can form inside the stems, obstructing the flow of water up to the flower. You can buy flower food from most flower shops and a small sachet (equivalent to approximately one large tablespoon) is enough for an average-sized vase.

Home-made flower food is just as effective, however. Mix equal quantities of water with a fizzy lemon drink and add 1½ teaspoons of household bleach. The fizzy drink contains sugar as a source of energy and citric acid that acts as an acidifier; the bleach keeps bacteria from forming in the water.

When using florist's foam, add the flower food to the water that the foam is to be soaked in (see below).

Using florist's foam

You can buy florist's foam from all florists and garden centres. There are two types: the one that is soaked in water and is usually green and quite soft; and the one that is used for dried or artificial flowers that doesn't soak up water and is usually grey. You can buy the foam in many shapes and sizes. The cheapest way to buy it is as a brick shape that you can then cut to the size you need using a sharp knife. Foam balls and rings are also available in various diameters. The most popular sizes for a ring are 25, 30, 35 and 40 cm (10, 12, 14 and 16 in).

Soak your foam thoroughly before using it and when inserting the flowers, always remember to put them in at an angle and not straight as this makes an arrangement look more natural. Remember, too, that foam dries just like a sponge – the top first – so make sure to water it every day to keep it wet. Do not use the same florist's foam twice, as used foam will not absorb water efficiently.

Wires

Wiring in floristry is a skilled job, and is used to make flowers stay in a particular shape – it is really only used when making wedding bouquets and buttonholes, for example. This book is all about flowers for the home and there is no formal wiring in any of the arrangements in the floristry sense of the word. The only times that wires are mentioned is to secure fruit or vegetables. In these cases you can use any firm wire bought from a hardware store, cut and bent into a hairpin shape. Alternatively, use cocktail or satay sticks, cut to size, and insert in the fruit.

Cementing in pots

If you are making a 'tree', and need to make the stem, take the twigs you are to use, and tie them securely at both ends with string. If you are using a valuable pot that you would like to re-use, cement the stems into a plastic container that can go inside the pot that is to be used. Use either quick-set cement or plaster of Paris. You can buy quick-set cement from any hardware or DIY store reasonably cheaply and you should mix it as described on the manufacturer's instructions. If using plaster of Paris, beware that if it gets wet, it has a musty smell!

Moss

Moss is bought from any florist. There are different types of moss, but for the arrangements used in this book, look for a fine variety. The moss can be bought and kept for a while, but take it out of the bag it comes in, or it can rot and become unpleasantly smelly.

Raffia, string and twine

Raffia can be bought from almost anywhere nowadays, as can string. In some of my arrangements I use twine, but if you can't get hold of this from a florist, use string or raffia instead. When choosing string, I prefer to use a heavily woven brand that looks hand-made because I feel that it looks better.

Using fruit and vegetables

Beware that rotting vegetables and fruit expel a gas called ethylene that will shorten the life of the flowers around it. It is therefore important to check that the fruit and vegetables are quite healthy and to change them once they begin to rot.

Containers

Any container that you think may work with flowers can be adapted for this use. The container is just as important as the arrangement and so I always think it is worth investing in good quality vases that will only add to your designs.

If using a container that is not 100 per cent waterproof, use a jam jar, cut down plastic bottle, glass or something similar that will fit inside the larger container. Likewise, if using florist's foam, it is best to line the container with plastic – cut it out from a bin liner or anything similar that comes to hand.

There are many lovely baskets around. My advice is to choose different, really interesting ones. There are too many cheap baskets used in floristry and a cheap basket can make the arrangement look cheap. So it really is worth investing in a good, solid basket if this is what you want for a particular arrangement.

Terracotta pots are lovely, too, and I am sure they will never be tired of, especially the old wonky ones. However, these have to be lined with a sheet of cellophane, a bin liner or any other waterproof material before filling with compost as they are not usually waterproof.

Spring

Tulips, grape hyacinths, daffodils – all spring flowers and all quite vibrant: flowers at this time of year are crying out to be arranged simply so that you can enjoy them to maximum effect.

SPRING

Topiary trees

When narcissi and daffodils are available in large quantities and they are cheap, too, it is fun to fill the house with them. Here is a wonderfully simple idea for a different way to arrange these spring flowers. The tall tumblers in which they are standing prevent the flowers from falling over and yet they still look rather stately.

Gather together a handful of narcissi or daffodils and arrange them in your hand so that the heads face outwards in all directions. To make sure the arrangement remains like this, tie a short length of the thin string or raffia at the top of the stems. It will be hidden by the flower heads. Then trim the stems as little as possible to the same length – the charm of this arrangement is that the stems remain long and elegant – and then place the bunches into tumblers of water, as in the photograph.

YOU WILL NEED:

Tall tumblers
Narcissi
Daffodils
Thin string or raffia

In addition to the narcissi and daffodils, the stems of a small bunch of parrot tulips have been trimmed short and they have been put into a plain glass container.

SPRING

Polianthus cups

The idea of using simple household containers works especially well with spring plants as container and flower alike are fresh and unpretentious. Using strong primary colours or softer, pastel tones, as here, you can group pots together to give an added splash of colour to your display.

Choose containers that are simple in shape and design. Strong coloured coffee mugs work well in this situation. If the containers don't have drainage, water them little but often, otherwise they can get waterlogged.

Plant the polianthus in the containers, making sure to wet their root balls well before planting them. Here, the plants have been deliberately planted so that the polianthus colour doesn't match the container. However, you might decide to match the plant with its pot to create a more ordered arrangement. The plants stand on a platter here, but you could just as easily arrange them in the centre of a table. The parrot tulips at the centre add a spot of variety and their additional height gives more shape to the arrangement.

YOU WILL NEED:

Assorted polianthus plants
Parrot tulips

The refreshingly bright shades of the polianthus plants combine beautifully with the slightly more muted shades of their containers.

SPRING

Blues and whites

Glass tanks look extremely smart but they are very often simply too large to fill with flowers. An ingenious solution is to place a smaller vase, drinking glass or plain jam jar, inside the tank and use that as a container for the flowers. The space around the small vase can be filled with eggs, smooth pebbles, glistening glass nuggets, shells from the seaside or any other small treasures. At Christmas time, fir cones and tree baubles could be used for a suitably festive look.

Here, duck eggs and quail eggs have been used, which are usually available from larger supermarkets or butchers. These come in a lovely range of soft, muted colours which complement the spring posy of flowers to perfection. Ordinary eggs work well, too, as they catch the light reflected off the glass. Eggs could even be painted with bright poster paints to match or contrast with the colours of the flowers being displayed – an activity in which you can enlist any keen young helpers.

Tulips, grape hyacinths and hyacinths have been used in this arrangement, but try other combinations such as tulips with jewel-coloured anemones and fat ranunculus buds. Remember to polish the tank well to ensure it is smear-free before filling it with eggs, and refresh the water every other day during the flowers' life.

YOU WILL NEED:

Large and small vases
Eggs (duck and quail)
Tulips
Muscari (grape hyacinths)
Hyacinths

A springtime selection of grape hyacinths, white tulips and rich purple hyacinths sits neatly in the corner of a large glass tank.

SPRING

Daffodil twig basket

Using daffodil and narcissi plants planted in a twig basket, you can make a lovely display that will last for a long time. To help encourage this longevity, water the plants often but sparingly, as the basket has no drainage and the plants can easily become waterlogged. Also, cut off the flower heads as they die. Not only will this keep the arrangement looking lovely and fresh, it will also give the plants strength to bring out the new flowers.

■ Twig baskets like this are available from any good florist or if you have easy access to a supply of twigs, make your own by bending the twigs into a circle and twisting the ends together. It is best to start with several larger twigs to make a firm base from which to build up. You may have to wire together the ends of these larger ones to keep them stable.

■ Line the basket with moss. This makes the finished arrangement look much softer and more complete. Then line the inside of the basket with some plastic to ensure that the soil from the plants and the water do not escape all over the surface on which you are intending to stand the display.

YOU WILL NEED:

Twig basket
All-purpose compost
Moss
Narcissi plants ('Sol d'or')
Daffodil plants ('Ice Folly')

■ Plant a generous group of the narcissi and daffodil plants in the twig basket in all-purpose compost, keeping the tallest at the back and the sides and working down to the smallest plants at the front. Fill any gaps in the basket with handfuls of compost so that the plants are well bedded in place.

■ To finish, insert twigs into the soil between the plants. This is both decorative and gives the whole design a suitably spring-like, woodlands look.

A large and welcoming arrangement like this would adorn any hallway.

SPRING

Mixed spring plants

Like the narcissi and daffodils that appear on pages 18-19, these spring flowers remain in soil so they will last for a good deal longer than if they were cut and put in water. Their container is essentially a shallow dish, but moss and twigs have been placed around the plants to prevent them from drying out and to make them look even more attractive.

The dish can be anything that you have in your kitchen, whether it be a soup plate or a slightly larger platter. Whatever you choose, it needs to have some depth to it so that the water doesn't run out too easily. Once you have created your arrangement, water it frequently, but not too much as there is no drainage and too much water can result in it being waterlogged. Cut off the dead flowers to keep the arrangement looking nice and to give the plants strength to bring out the new blooms.

Take your selection of spring plants and remove their pots, having first given the plants a good soaking with water. Place them on the dish so that they are positioned close to each other and arranged how you will want to view them. Surround the plants with a layer of moss that is built up to the height of the soil. This helps keep the moisture in as well as being decorative, and then surround with fine, small twigs from the garden to help keep the plants from drooping as they grow. Finally, tie the arrangement all around with twine, raffia or string, positioning it just above the moss.

YOU WILL NEED:

Narcissi plants ('Sol d'or')
Tulip plants
Muscari (grape hyacinth) plants
Hyacinth plants
Dish
Moss
Twine, raffia or string

The beauty of flowers is that no matter what colour they are, they combine well. Here the red, blue and yellow create a refreshing, spring arrangement.

SPRING

Tin pot amaryllis

Choosing old, unusual containers can turn the simplest of designs into something special. The ivy that surrounds the base of the plants adds texture and a variation in scale to the whole arrangement. Plant the amaryllis in an all-purpose compost but if the container has no drainage, it is essential to use bulb-fibre instead. Here, five plants have been grouped together, but you may find that your container has room for more or fewer. Whatever quantity you are using, it is always best to use an odd number of plants as the finished arrangement looks much freer in this way. After planting the flowers, add the ivy, draping it gracefully around the flowers and over the edges of the container.

If your container has no drainage, make sure to water it often but sparingly so that it doesn't become waterlogged. If amaryllis plants aren't to your taste or aren't available, this idea works just as well with many other spring plants, such as hyacinths and tulips. However, bear in mind the size of your plants when choosing your container – anything too large can easily swamp smaller plants like these. It is the height of the amaryllis plants that enables you to use a larger, more solid container like the one featured in the photograph.

YOU WILL NEED:

Tin container
All-purpose compost
5 white amaryllis plants
Ivy

White, green and grey – here is a strikingly simple combination of colours arranged for maximum effect.

SPRING

Tulips and bamboo

Bulb flowers are rather heavy, and so can droop all too easily. Using simple sticks and raffia, as in the picture opposite, you are not only preventing them from going over, but also making a feature out of supporting them. For something even more colourful, use one of the brightly coloured raffias that are available.

Plant a generous number of tulip plants (or other bulb flowers) in a terracotta pot and cover the top with a thin layer of moss to prevent the soil from drying out too rapidly. Then cut down four bamboo sticks to an appropriate length, push the ends into the soil, and tie the raffia around them, surrounding the plants. Here, the bamboo is the same height as the plants, but you might prefer to make them shorter and have more of them. You could then weave the raffia in and out of the bamboo canes to create a woven basket effect around the tulip stems. A short length of raffia has been tied around this particular terracotta pot as a neat and decorative finish.

YOU WILL NEED:

Tulip plants
Terracotta pot
Bamboo canes
Moss
Raffia

The raffia-entwined bamboo is not only a decorative adornment, it is also highly practical as it prevents the heavy tulip heads from drooping.

24

SPRING

Spring posy

Many people are afraid of mixing colours, in case they don't match. But mixing together many strong spring colours usually works really well, especially if there is a little foliage separating the flowers.

YOU WILL NEED:

Narcissi (yellow)
Muscari (grape hyacinths)
Tulips (white)
Ranunculus (cerise)
Foliage
String, ribbon or raffia

■ Strip the surplus leaves off all the flowers and discard them. Then lay out the flowers on your worksurface. Don't worry about ordering them in any way as you will, after all, be creating a mixed posy.

■ Gather them together, one by one, mixing in foliage with flowers, and twisting the posy round as you work. This will ensure that you end up with a rounded, domed shape and also that the flowers are evenly spread around the posy.

■ Tie together the stems with string, ribbon or raffia, and cut all the stems to the same length to give a very neat finish.

If you are giving away this posy, wrap it up in several layers of tissue paper. Choose a colour that tones in with the flowers.

SPRING

Pink, cream and green

The long spikes of moluccella and variegated pittosporum look wonderful sprouting above the wax flowers and pink tulips and hyacinths in this arrangement. The common names for moluccella are Bells of Ireland or shell flower and when you look closely at the calyx that surrounds each tiny white flower it is easy to see why. This plant is quite dramatic in its own right but when combined with something a little softer in shape it makes for a most attractive design.

Wax flowers also form a part of this arrangement. These flowers are becoming increasingly popular as cut flowers and their scented blooms growing in clusters fit in with many a spring arrangement. Try not to use them in arrangements that are too large, however, as the small flowers can all too easily be swamped. In this design, they look especially good because they complement the hyacinths both in scale and colour, contrasting with the larger tulip heads.

Prepare the flowers for this arrangement by stripping off the leaves from the lower parts of the stems and group them in your container. Make sure that the moluccella spikes appear at random intervals around the edges and not in groups – the architectural nature of these plants would only detract from the overall softness if they were grouped together.

YOU WILL NEED:

Moluccella
Pittosporum (variegated)
Hyacinths (pink)
Tulips (pink)
Wax flowers

Pale pinks and green are grouped informally for a simple springtime arrangement.

Summer

A time of abundance, when flower shops, market stalls and gardens are filled to bursting point with blooms in an inspiring array of colours.

SUMMER

Lemons and sunflowers

For a fresh and wonderfully original design, fill a bowl with fruit before arranging the summer flowers in it. The container that has been used here is a clear glass salad bowl and it has been filled with lemons which have a very fresh summery look. They also tone in with the sunflowers quite spectacularly well.

YOU WILL NEED:
Clear glass salad bowl
Fruit (lemons)
Clear plastic sheet
Florist's foam
Sunflowers
Roses (orange)
Freesias (purple)
Foliage
Satay sticks (optional)

■ Place the fruit around the bowl leaving as large a space as possible in the centre – if the bowl is not very big, you may have to cut the fruit in half to fit them in.

■ Place a film of clear plastic or cellophane in the centre of the bowl between the fruit, and then cut a piece of wet florist's foam to fit. Allow the florist's foam to be higher than the rim of the bowl.

■ You are now able to arrange your flowers in the florist's foam. To follow the fruity theme through the design, consider adding some lemons (or whatever fruit you have filled the base with) to the flower arrangement. To do this, take a satay stick or similar, insert it in the fruit and secure the other end of the stick in the florist's foam.

■ Top up the water of the florist's foam frequently so that it doesn't dry up. If the fruits in the arrangement begin to rot, take them out and replace with new ones straight away. Rotting fruits expel a gas (ethelyne) that can shorten the life of the flowers.

Fruit and flowers may be an unusual combination, but this way of making a large glass vase look a little different works exceptionally well.

32

SUMMER

Blue and purple jugs

Summer flowers look extremely beautiful arranged in an informal way in simple, household containers such as teapots and jugs. Choose soft summer flowers and mix them with garden foliage, stripping the leaves that would otherwise be below water level. Not only will rotting leaves start smelling pretty awful, they will also hasten the end of your arrangement.

Fill up the containers by first putting in the foliage to give your display its basic shape, and then add the flowers. The beauty of the arrangements in this photograph is their naturalness, so don't feel that you need to force the flowers into a more formal collection. Instead, allow them to tumble gracefully in all directions, and especially to flow over the edges of the containers to keep all edges soft and blowsy. Float any surplus buds and flower heads in a saucer of water.

To help keep the arrangement fresh, put flower food in the water (see page 8) or change the water daily.

YOU WILL NEED:

Mixture of containers
***Viburnum opulus* (guelder rose)**
Agapanthus (blue)
Anemones (blue)
Mexican orange bush
Delphiniums
Few sprigs of rosemary

Summery blues and greens combine in a flourish for an informal, light arrangement fresh from the garden.

34

SUMMER

Lisianthus wreath

When making a ring of fresh flowers, it is very effective to use one type of flower only, and in one colour only. Here, white lisianthus alone has been used to fill up a florist's foam ring. Lisianthus is also known as eustoma and it is a poppy-like plant that is also available in pink or blue. If lisianthus isn't around, think about using freesias which can be bought in similar colours.

Cut the stems of the flowers that you have chosen to around 10 cm (4 in), and insert them well into the florist's foam. Start from the centre and work outwards and always try to put them in sideways, never straight up, to avoid a stiff finish to the wreath.

If you are going to use the wreath on a door, hang it up from some raffia tied around the top of the florist's foam ring. Alternatively, use it as a ring to put on a table, surrounding the base of a candelabra. Remember to water the florist's foam every day, as it will dry out.

YOU WILL NEED:
25 cm (10 in) diameter florist's foam ring
Lisianthus (white)
Raffia

A design made from one colour alone is truly simple and very refreshing. The wreath makes the most striking of door decorations.

SUMMER

Tree and napkin ring

Take an old pot, some twigs, a florist's foam ball and summer flowers and you can create a really stunning arrangement for a summer lunch party. Order the florist's foam ball from a florist or use a piece of wet florist's foam cut into a semi-rounded shape. For a spot of co-ordination, small bunches of flowers have been made to wrap around the napkins.

■ Secure a generous group of twigs into a pot using either plaster, quick-set cement or dried florist's foam bricks weighted down with stones. The best of these options is cement as the plaster can smell if it gets wet, and the florist's foam and stones may not make it secure enough. Leave the cement to dry.

■ Tie the twigs securely at the top with some twine. Then cut the twigs to one length, and secure the ball of wet florist's foam on the top. So that the florist's foam does not slide down the stems, wire a small group of twigs around the vertical twigs, towards the top.

■ Cut down the flowers and foliage and insert them into the florist's foam, making sure to cover the ball completely and evenly.

YOU WILL NEED:
Terracotta pots (1 medium-sized and several smaller ones)
Twigs
Plaster, quick-set cement or florist's foam
Twine
15 cm (6 in) diameter florist's foam ball
Moss
Roses (red and pink)
Matricaria
Scabius
Alchemilla
Solidago
Cornflowers
Variegated pittosporum
Galax leaves
Raffia
Candles

■ Cover the base of the pot with moss.

■ To make the matching napkin rings, take a few of the flowers and leaves, tie them into bunches and then tie them around the rolled-up napkins with raffia.

■ Finally, put candles in the smaller terracotta pots, securing them in place with moss.

Candle pots are arranged around the elegant rose and alchemilla tree, and the floral napkin rings finish off the dining table to make a charmingly co-ordinated setting.

SUMMER

Candle centrepiece

Summer gives many an opportunity for dining al fresco and on especially still days candlelight adds considerably to the atmosphere. This particular centrepiece has been created from an old piece of wood (taken from a rotting piece of fence in the garden!), broken to the required length. In the photograph, it is 50 cm (20 in) long. Holes the diameter of the candle have been drilled into the piece of wood, and candles put in the holes.

To complete the informal look, and making fresh and lovely napkin rings at the same time, take flowers from the garden and tie them together with a little raffia. Leave the strands of raffia long enough to tie around a rolled-up napkin. This same idea could also be used for adorning the wooden candle holder, swathing it with raffia-tied bunches of flowers. Of course, the flowers wouldn't last for long so make this the last thing you do before your guests arrive. To finish off, take a small flower vase and fill it with a very simple flower arrangement.

YOU WILL NEED:

Old piece of wood
Candles
Primulas
Pansies
Hydrangeas
Matricaria
Raffia

Outdoor living is easy and carefree so don't spoil it with a complicated flower arrangement – simple, small groupings are best.

SUMMER

Pastel pots and roses

Working only with pastel colours can be very effective, especially if your design is kept very simple. Here, for example, the colours of the roses match the colours of the pots quite perfectly, and they have then been grouped together to achieve a soft summer look.

Buy your roses while they are in bud and during the few days that it will take for them to open up, paint your pots and saucers with matt emulsion to match the shades of your roses. Small pots of emulsion mixed to the colour of your choice are readily available. When the paint is dry, line the pots with plastic or cellophane, and put pieces of cut-down florist's foam in the pots, making sure the florist's foam is taller than the rim of the pot.

Cutting down the rose stems as necessary, arrange the flowers in each pot of its same colour, making an untidy ball and placing strands of ivy between to complete the informal look. Water the florist's foam frequently – as the pieces are small, they will dry up quite quickly.

YOU WILL NEED:

Old plant pots and saucers
Matt emulsion paint
Paintbrush
Plastic sheeting
Florist's foam
Roses in the following varieties:
'Stirling Silver' (lilac)
'Oceana' (peach)
'Limona' (yellow)
'Valery' (pink)
Ivy

Shades of pastel pink, peach and yellow roses and pots combine to make a beautiful and fragrant collection.

SUMMER

Citrus fruits and flowers

The basis of this design is simple, everyday fruits the colours of which have been matched with citric-coloured flowers, and large, shapely foliage. Oranges and limes contrast so beautifully colourwise, and yet complement each other in terms of shape and texture. They form the core of this arrangement and everything else has been chosen to co-ordinate with these fruits. Such a bold and chunky design would be most striking on a side table in a dining room or kitchen.

■ Line the old terracotta pot with plastic or cellophane to prevent any water from leaking out. Terracotta pots tend not to be waterproof.

■ Cut a piece of florist's foam to fit inside the lining, making sure it is a little taller than the rim of the pot.

■ Using satay sticks to secure the fruit to the florist's foam (see page 9), position the fruits all around the pot in an informal, irregular arrangement. Leave spaces all around for the flowers and foliage.

■ Add the flowers and foliage, remembering to insert them at an angle to give the design a softer, more flowing look.

■ Water the florist's foam frequently and also check regularly that the fruit isn't rotting. This can happen quite quickly as it is in contact with a wet surface. If it is rotting, change it immediately, as rotting fruit emits ethylene gas that is harmful to the longevity of flowers.

YOU WILL NEED:

Terracotta pot
Plastic sheeting
Florist's foam
Oranges
Limes
Satay sticks
Orange roses ('Julia')
***Viburnum opulus* ('Snowball')**
Ranunculus (orange)
Gaultiera leaves
Variegated pittosporum

Small flower heads of roses, ranunculus and viburnum nestle among the more dramatic backdrop of limes, oranges and large, shiny gaultiera leaves.

Autumn

Many summer flowers continue to grow well into autumn with shades of orange, russet and brown predominating. So bring the autumnal colours indoors and enjoy the harvest splendours.

AUTUMN

The dinner table

When the centre of the dinner table is taken up by a large platter or candelabra, for example, add floral decorations in the form of small individual flower arrangements next to each place setting. This works especially well for a small dinner party as the table can look too fussy with many small arrangements if the dinner party is any larger than six people.

Each arrangement is made in a small terracotta pot. Keep an eye out for old ones as these are so much more attractive – their weathered patina softens the outline – and once you have pots like this you will find ways to use them again and again for different arrangements. Also, if you can find small terracotta saucers to go under the pots, the arrangements look so much more finished off, especially if they are to sit on a smart tablecloth.

Line each pot with plastic or cellophane to prevent water leaking out of the bottom, and place a piece of florist's foam cut to size inside, making sure that it is a little taller than the rim of the pot. Then add the flowers, foliage and fruit. In the case of the small fruit used here, it is best to secure them to the florist's foam using either wires or small toothpicks (see page 9). If lychees are available, use these too; they look great near the smooth grapes as their textures contrast so strongly.

YOU WILL NEED:
Small terracotta pots
Plastic sheeting
Florist's foam
Mustard-coloured small roses ('Safari')
Grapes
Autumn foliage

This arrangement is the essence of autumn with its deep, purply reds and shades of terracotta and yellow.

48

AUTUMN

Burgundy and orange bouquet

Here is a truly striking bouquet that has been created by choosing just two unusual colours of roses that are combined with a similarly deep-coloured foliage. The lack of green foliage means that the bouquet retains a striking and wonderfully rich mass. The ornamental peppers bring some variety to the arrangement through their shiny, smooth surface – quite a contrast against the velvety rose petals.

Use roses that are just beginning to open out and trim the stems (see page 8) to an appropriate length. Remove any leaves from the lower parts of the stems. Wire the ornamental peppers as described on page 9. Gather the roses, cotinus leaves and peppers into the palm of your hand, one by one, turning the bouquet around as you go in order to get a very rounded shape. Once you are happy with the shape and size of the bouquet, tie together the arrangement beneath the flower heads. Then cut the stems to the same height and place them in a vase with a small neck.

YOU WILL NEED:

Roses ('Black Magic' and 'Pareo')
Cotinus leaves
Orange ornamental peppers
Twine
Florist's wire
Narrow necked vase

A bouquet that features no green foliage looks very dense because there is no lighter shade to break up its shape.

50

AUTUMN

Vegetable vase

A striking glass vase containing autumn-coloured flowers, berries and foliage sounds wonderful in itself. But when the vase is also filled with orange peppers and deep purple aubergines, the end result is quite splendid – and definitely unique.

Fill your large glass vase with the fruit and vegetables of your choice, but keep it simple otherwise the design looks too fussy. Work on a good contrast of colour that will match the flowers used in the arrangement. Although orange peppers and aubergines were used here, you could just as easily go for, say, green or red peppers combined with cooking apples. Hunt around for interesting combinations of shapes, colours and textures; combine smooth and shiny vegetables or unite a rough texture with a glossy piece of fruit. It is great fun deciding what to use, and you can make it different each time.

As you fill the vase, make sure that you leave sufficient space in the middle for a smaller glass or vase to fit in. Position it in the vase making sure that it is secure, fill it with water and then arrange the flowers in it.

YOU WILL NEED:

Large glass vase
Smaller glass or vase
Orange peppers
Aubergines
Euphorbia (orange)
Orange roses ('Pareo')
Burgundy roses ('Black Magic')
Cotinus foliage
Choisia

Mix and match – not only are the flowers in autumnal shades, but so are the contents of the vase. The end result is a unified and glossy design.

AUTUMN

Amaryllis in a long tom pot

When using a long thin vase, the natural idea is to use long stemmed flowers and foliage. However, in this arrangement, proportions have been played around with by cutting the flowers short so that they are just about peeping over the rim of the pot. Try the same idea in the spring with masses of daffodils or at any time of the year with roses.

If you are using a terracotta vase as a container, put a smaller glass or plastic vase inside (a cut-up large size soft drink bottle is quite useful!) as most terracotta is not waterproof. If the terracotta is new, you can tone it down by slightly whitewashing it. To do this, sponge a very small amount of white emulsion mixed with lots of water all over the surface and leave to dry. Arrange the amaryllis one by one in the pot, cutting as needed so that the stems in the centre of the design are slightly longer than those around the edge. This will give a beautifully round shape to the arrangement.

YOU WILL NEED:

Tall terracotta vase
Amaryllis stems (orange)

The long and short of it is that the massed flower heads of the amaryllis stems merge into one large, magnificent whole.

AUTUMN

Be-decked tool box

This battered old wooden box makes a wonderful container for a bold and chunky design featuring autumn vegetables and fruits. The rich tones of deep red, purple and green interspersed with the occasional pale pink wax flower for a lighter touch, combine for a truly autumnal feel. Harvest and Thanksgiving are approaching.

Line an old wooden box with plastic or cellophane to prevent water leakage, and then fill it with florist's foam. Ensure that the florist's foam is higher than the rim of the box. First arrange the shiny green and dark foliage, and then add vegetables and fruit, and finally the flowers. When you are inserting the vegetables, either wire them or use satay sticks (see page 9) and then start with the largest pieces first. Here the artichokes, for example, have been positioned one at each end of the box and the rest of the fruits and vegetables arranged around them. To prevent the design from becoming too formal, make sure that the dominant features like the artichokes are inserted at different angles.

Water the foam often to prevent it drying up. Also check the fruit and vegetables regularly to see if there is any sign of rotting. If so, remove and replace the offending items as they will emit ethylene gas, which is harmful to the longevity of the flowers.

YOU WILL NEED:

Old wooden box
Plastic sheeting
Florist's foam
Red Spanish onions
Artichokes
Plums
Wire or satay sticks
Tulips (dark red)
Galax leaves
Rhodedendron foliage
Wax flowers (pink)

A bold arrangement is very quick to put together; the skill comes in choosing the ingredients in the first place.

AUTUMN

Oranges and lemons

By using a simple mixture of citrus fruit, you will get a very sunny wreath any time of the year! This arrangement is simple, to make, and only lasts for a couple of weeks – so it is only worth doing for a very special occasion! It is also very heavy, so make sure the hook from which it is going to hang is quite secure. To complement the wreath, make candle and simple lemon arrangements by using the same system of dried florist's foam, and fruit supported by satay sticks with foliage between.

For preparation, take all the oranges and lemons, and insert a satay stick into each so that only 5 cm (2 in) protrudes from the bottom. Also strip down a few short pieces of euonymus and ruscus.

Then take your foam ring but do not wet it or the fruit will rot very quickly (the foliage has been chosen specifically because it will last a few weeks without water). Insert the oranges, lemons and foliage, always putting in the satay sticks and stems at an angle to keep the arrangement looking soft and fluid. Ensure that the foam is entirely covered and then hang it from a wire or length of string. To finish off, tie a small ball of kumquats to the end of the string.

YOU WILL NEED:

25-30 cm (10-12 in) diameter florist's foam ring
Satay sticks
Oranges
Lemons
Ruscus
Variegated euonymus
Kumquats

Oranges and lemons are combined in a simple and bright arrangement that will stay looking good for a few weeks.

58

AUTUMN

Autumn rust

Match autumn colours by using rusty containers with rust-coloured flowers. Choose old, household objects like an old loaf tin, a wire egg basket and a rusty urn, and line with plastic or cellophane. If the object has lots of gaps in it, like the egg basket used here, line it with moss for an attractive finish. Then fill the containers with florist's foam cut to the right size making sure that the pieces come up over the rims.

Fill the containers with interesting foliage and flowers, and water them frequently so that the florist's foam does not dry up. In the photograph opposite, the urn is filled with cotinus leaves and leonidas roses, and the egg basket contains parrot tulips and variegated ivy leaves. Finally, the rudbekia, protea, hypericum berries, ivy berries and the red huckleberry foliage fill the old loaf tin. It is important that you arrange similar scaled pieces together so that one flower doesn't swamp another.

YOU WILL NEED:

Cotinus leaves
Leonidas roses
Parrot tulips
Variegated ivy leaves
Rudbekia
Protea
Hypericum berries
Ivy berries
Huckleberry foliage

Bring shades of autumn into your home, setting them in rusty containers to echo the warm, fiery colours.

AUTUMN

AUTUMN

Harvest time

Harvest is a time of abundance and also a time of rich, autumnal shades. Here the two themes are united in an arrangement featuring very simple everyday vegetables – such as potatoes, cabbages, turnips, and lychees – mixed in with flowers in russets and greens, with the occasional blue flower head to act as an accent in the design.

To prevent the arrangement from looking too heavy and symmetrical, try to use fruit and vegetables of different shapes and sizes as you build it up. The addition of foliage, and in particular ivy, all through to the top, also softens the cone, preventing it from becoming a stiff and unforgiving shape.

■ Gather dried straight twigs, and cut them all to the same height and approximately to the height you would like the arrangement to be. Tie them securely at both ends with twine and cement one end of the sticks into the old terracotta pot (see page 9). Make sure that the cement reaches the rim of the top, or top it up with moss or florist's foam.

■ Begin the arrangement by sitting a few large pieces of fruit or vegetables on the pot, around the twig stem. So that they don't topple off, tie them loosely to the stem using a piece of the wire (see page 9).

■ In the gaps between this layer of fruit or vegetables, insert little squares of wet florist's foam, into which you can arrange foliage and flowers, as you wish.

■ Build a second layer in the same way and continue to work your way up the pot, using increasingly small fruit, vegetables, flowers and greenery, until you finish at the top of the cone.

YOU WILL NEED:

Twigs

Twine

Quick-set cement

Old terracotta pot

Wire

Florist's foam

Red roses ('Black Magic')

Orange roses ('Pareo')

Protea heads

Anemones (blue)

Ivy and other foliage

Various fruit and vegetables (potatoes, cabbages, turnips, lychees, passion fruit, kumquats, physalis fruit, red onions, mushrooms, mini aubergines)

The knobbly kumquats and physalis fruit next to the smoother rose petals and shiny red onion skin make this arrangement a textural delight.

62

Winter

Choose to echo the bareness of the trees with twiggy, sparse arrangements, or bring some colour back into your life with brightly coloured flowers. With flowers imported from all over the world, there is never any shortage of blooms in the shops

WINTER

Metallic shades

The mixture of acid-coloured roses in a metal container creates a sharp, modern design that works well in a contemporary background. The end result is cool and striking because the colours have been combined in such an unusual way. Choose strong coloured flowers, keeping the combination simple (no more than three colours works best). Colours that work well for this acid look are strident orange, shocking pink, and strong yellow or lime green.

Take your metal container (the one used here is a galvanized coal scooper) and fill it with wet florist's foam that is slightly higher than the rim. Then arrange the flowers loosely, trimming the stems as necessary and stripping off any foliage that will be in the water. Make sure that the arrangement isn't too symmetrical or the design will start to look too heavy. Fill the gaps between the roses with generous amounts of dark green ivy allowing the occasional tendril to drift down the side of the container. The ivy adds an architectural touch to the design and the small leaves a refreshing variation in scale. Top up the arrangement with water frequently so that it lasts as long as possible.

YOU WILL NEED:

Metal container
Florist's foam
Orange roses ('Pareo')
Pink roses ('Ravel')
Yellow roses ('Texas')
Ivy

A cool-coloured arrangement for cool winter days. Such strikingly coloured blossoms are softened by the ivy detail that meanders through the arrangement.

WINTER

Orchids and willow

Orchids can look very grand and formal – but mixed with lots of tortured willow and put into an old rusted fire bucket, they are transformed into a more modern and fun design. This is due to the contrast between the traditionally luxurious plant such as an orchid and its old, battered container.

Fill the bucket with the light soil and then plant the three phalaenopsis orchids. Orchids are semi-aerial plants, and need hardly any soil, so do not pack them in too tightly. The stems of orchids are usually held up by a pole, but for this arrangement they have been replaced with the stems of tortured willow. To add some more style and to soften the design, yet more tortured willow has been inserted into the soil around the orchids. Tortured willow works well when using generous amounts – if you are too restrained, you can end up with an old-fashioned *ikebana* design!

To keep the orchids fresh, mist them with water frequently from a sprayer, and water them every couple of days very sparingly. They need a lot of moisture so that their buds don't dry up before flowering.

YOU WILL NEED:

Old bucket
Light soil
3 white phalaenopsis orchids
Tortured willow

The tortured willow weaves its way gracefully in and out and around about the tall and stately orchid plants.

WINTER

White simplicity

Abundance and simplicity are the key to this classic flower arrangement which would look good in any setting, formal or informal. Approximately 30 or so large white lily stems were used to fill up this vase, with almost the same amount of foliage. Of course, lilies can look just wonderful on their own, but with the large quantities of shiny green foliage emerging from between the flower heads, this arrangement is most fulsome.

Trim the lily and foliage stems as described on page 8 ensuring that they are of a similar length and also strip the stems of any foliage that would otherwise be in water. Put them into the vase, one by one, mixing the lilies and foliage in equal quantities. Add flower food or keep the water clean by changing it daily (see page 8).

YOU WILL NEED:

Pompeii lilies
Gaultiera leaves

The white flower heads and green foliage make a striking and yet extremely successful contrasting arrangement.

WINTER

Stone-filled vase

To give added interest to an arrangement, fill a glass tank with stones before adding the flowers. Make sure you wash the stones thoroughly in water with a little bleach added before putting them in the vase. The dirt on the stones could otherwise cloud the water as well as be harmful to the longevity of the flowers. Then arrange the flowers in a simple hand-tied bouquet, gathering the stems in your hand, one by one, and turning the bouquet around as you add to it. Cut the stems to fit between the stones, and secure them with a few more stones around the edge. Top up with water often.

Not all pebbles are grey, of course, and depending on where you go for your pebbles you can find many a variation on white, yellow, red and black. Search for interestingly veined and mottled pebbles always bearing in mind that when a pebble is wet its colours become richer. So as you stroll along that beach, take a small bucket of water with you.

Finding flowers to contrast with the pebbles is fun, too. Here the grey and white shades co-ordinate subtly, but if you find white pebbles you might prefer to choose some brighter colour of bloom like a fat ranunculus or two, or some purple and red anemones. A yellower stone might combine well with deeper autumn shades.

YOU WILL NEED:

White roses ('Bianca')
Brunei protea heads
Viburnum berries
Ivy
Variegated pittosporum
Eucalyptus

Stones in the bottom of a clear glass vase add just a little extra to a flower arrangement. Here the grey pebbles contrast beautifully with the white roses above.

WINTER

Silver candelabra

For a formal dinner setting, decorate the base of a candelabra with a ring of winter flowers, and for each place setting, arrange a few flowers in a small silver cup. Plenty of variegated ivy has been used as this lightens the arrangement.

From a florist, buy the smallest florist's foam ring that your candelabra will be able to sit in – usually a diameter of 25 cm (10 in) is sufficient. Wet the foam and then add the flowers, always inserting them at an angle, and using lots of foliage between. Add the grapes in big clumps, simply securing them loosely with wire hairpins (see page 9). Do the same with the plums, but inserting them singly rather than in groups. Finally, add sprigs of ivy to soften the wreath shape, and with what ivy is left over, twirl lengths up the candelabra so that the arrangement looks as though it is all one.

If you have some very small silver bowls, make individual place setting arrangements in some florist's foam that will match the candelabra and ring of flowers, but keep them small and simple. Here, three rose heads have been combined with a handful of the leaves and just a few grapes inserted to finish off. This is a charming way to complete a table setting.

YOU WILL NEED:

25 cm (10 in) diameter florist's foam ring
Wire
Red roses ('Black Magic')
Black grapes
Dark plums
Gaultiera leaves
Hebe leaves/variegated ivy

As it is so easy to gather great swathes of ivy, collect much more than you need and then you can use the best bits.

WINTER

Primary shades

For a fun, colourful setting, choose small bright, different coloured vases and fill with strong coloured flowers, trying to keep as close as possible to primary colours. Here, seven different coloured containers were chosen. You could use cups or small bowls; these ones are really night light holders bought from a candle shop. Fill them with florist's foam cut to size so that the top of the foam reaches just below the rim of the containers.

So that the flowers aren't overpowered by the vases, choose strong coloured flowers, prepare them as described on page 8, and put them into the florist's foam, one by one, always at an angle. Do not make each arrangement too big or the pots will be hidden.

Place the arrangements either at the centre of the table in a ring (as in the photograph), or arranged in a long row down the middle of the table. In between, use little night lights dotted around them. If you can find ones in coloured metal containers, all the better. So that the colours show up well, use a white tablecloth as a base but bring out any coloured bottles, bright cutlery and glasses that you may own, and the table setting really will be a splash of fun colours.

YOU WILL NEED:

Anemones (red and purple)
Tulips (yellow, purple, orange and variegated)

For the brightest of shades, look for anemones and tulips, as here, or search for ranunculus, freesias and lisimachia, which glow just as successfully.

WINTER

Symmetrical fireplace

Sometimes the simplest of ideas work best. Here is a large fireplace and it has been decorated simply and yet quite dramatically with two large terracotta pots filled to overflowing with large bunches of just one type of flower.

Take two old terracotta pots and place a smaller, ordinary glass or vase inside each one into which you will put the flowers. Position the vases so that their tops appear just over the rim of the pot. Take your bunches of camomile flowers, cut them down carefully, so that you are left with short stems and masses of flower heads. Then gather up the flowers, one by one, in your hand, twisting the bunch round as you add to it to ensure you get an even and round shape at the end. Put the bunches into the vases inside the pots. Add flower food or change the water every day to ensure longevity. Finish off each vase with a generous bow of raffia tied around the flower stems.

YOU WILL NEED:

Two terracotta pots
Two small vases
Camomile (matricaria) flowers
Raffia

Pots filled with generous quantities of the same flower have a very luxurious quality. Put a smaller container inside the larger one and you will need to use fewer flowers, but end up with the same result.

78

WINTER

WINTER

Leafy vases

Instead of having leaves coming out of vases, why not show off the leaves and the shape of the vase, by keeping them in the container itself? This idea is truly original and with the striking foliage that is now available, you can create the most extraordinary effects, as shown in the photograph opposite.

It is essential that your vase is spotlessly clean before putting anything into it as smeary finger marks and any remnants of dust will undoubtedly show up. Once it is clean, place the leaves in the vase, making sure to use only a few and interesting leaves otherwise it looks like a cluttered mess. These designs only work well if you can see through them. In these vases I have used the palm leaf in the first vase followed by bear grass, monstera leaves and, finally, the butterfly leaves.

Once you have organised your leaves, add clean water to the vase and also a very small drop of bleach, to keep the leaves from rotting. It is especially important with this design idea that you change the water daily. As we all know, leaves rot in water fairly quickly, but with the bleach and a frequent change of water, these unusual arrangements can last for well over a week.

YOU WILL NEED:

Palm leaves
Bear grass
Monstera leaves
Butterfly leaves

Possibly the simplest of ideas to be found in this book, the architectural quality of these leaves is incredibly satisfying.

Special Occasions

Make special arrangements for those special occasions. Christmas and Valentine's day immediately spring to mind, but how about Halloween, a birthday, or to accompany some delicious canapés?

SPECIAL OCCASIONS

Valentine's heart

We all love to give or receive flowers on Valentine's Day and this ivy-trimmed heart of plush red roses makes a perfect romantic gift. The basic idea can be adapted for other occasions and the wreath would look equally stunning filled with pink roses for a summer table, or with white winter roses for Christmas.

YOU WILL NEED:

Chicken wire
Protective gloves
Moss
Plastic sheeting
Florist's foam
20 red roses ('Grand Gala')
Ivy
Twigs
Raffia or string

■ Wearing protective gloves, cut a 30 cm (12 in) square out of chicken wire and turn in the edges, rolling each towards the middle, filling them with a generous amount of moss as you go. You will end up with a square of chicken wire with a 'sausage' of moss all around the sides.

■ Carefully work the square into a heart shape by pulling the two top corners of the square into the top of the heart and shaping the rest from there until you get the heart shape.

■ In the space left in the centre, place a little moss at the bottom, and then line the moss with plastic or cellophane. Finally, place a piece of wet florist's foam in the middle. Surround the foam with moss so that it fits in quite securely.

■ Cut the rose stems to 10 cm (4 in) and position them in the foam to form a heart shape. Work around the outside edge first and then fill in the middle.

■ To accentuate the heart shape of the chicken wire, add twigs, tying them onto the chicken wire with raffia or string.

■ Finally, to soften the look, put ivy all around the heart shape.

The perfect Valentine's day gift – a heart-shaped wreath filled with velvety red roses.

SPECIAL OCCASIONS

Christmas wreath

A Christmas door wreath does not have to be the traditional ring shape with apples, cinammon sticks and tartan ribbon! Instead, why not make this design which is in the shape of an untidy, elongated heart, with red and white decorations?

■ Gather or buy 1 m (1 yd) long twigs, trim them to a similar length and divide into two equal sized bundles. Cross over the bundles at one end and tie them tightly with twine. Then bend them out and tie securely at the bottom in the same way, making an elongated heart shape.

■ Add more twine and twigs to the shape. Also, tie together bunches of the fake berries and attach these to the base. You will end up with a much fuller shape and don't worry about making it neat and tidy – the essence of this design is its informal untidiness.

■ At irregular intervals, and using the red gingham ribbon, tie the flowers to the wreath. The flowers used in the photograph are stripy red and white roses that match the gingham ribbon. Change the roses as they wilt.

■ An alternative is to fill small metal buckets with florist's foam, insert the roses and tie the buckets to the wreath. Water the buckets at frequent intervals.

YOU WILL NEED:
Twigs
Twine
Fake berries
Gingham ribbons
Stripy roses ('Matisse')
Small metal buckets (optional)
Florist's foam (for the buckets)

Don't feel that you must restrict yourself to roses in this wreath. Depending on the season, you may wish to use other flowers such as lavender, heather or daffodils in the spring.

SPECIAL OCCASIONS

Leafy wrapping paper

An unusual way to wrap up presents is by using real leaves and flowers and for wrapping up the odd present once in a while, it's great fun and certainly different. Always wrap them up at the last minute so that the leaves do not wilt. Order your tropical leaves from a flower shop and keep them in a cool place until you are ready to wrap up your gift.

First wrap your present with plain brown paper. Then select your leaves – you need to use ones that are not too fleshy as they will wilt quickly and are difficult to bend around the corners of the package. Leave them to turn a little limp and dry them thoroughly. Place strong double-sided tape on the back of the leaves, and put them on the brown paper present, one by one, trying to follow the shape of the present with the leaves. Different shaped packages will demand different ways of dealing with the leaves. For example, in the photograph opposite, a tall cylinder has been wrapped with long leaves that are left open at the top, looking rather plant-like. Smaller parcels will mean that leaves will need folding over each other.

To finish, tie up your present with a natural twine, string, raffia or even long grasses. Green garden string also looks good. At the last moment, also consider adding a little bunch of flowers instead of a bow. Keep the whole package cool until present-giving time.

YOU WILL NEED:

Plain brown paper
Double-sided tape
Assortment of tropical leaves
Matricaria
Roses
Viburnum opulus
Hydrangea flowers
Foliage
Natural twine, string or raffia

Leaves are an exotic and truly unusual way of wrapping gifts. A small bunch of flowers adds a colourful finishing touch.

88

SPECIAL OCCASIONS

Halloween pumpkin

Here is a fun way of cutting a pumpkin so that it looks bald and dressing it up with oranges decked with flowers and candles. The arrangements to each side are made especially autumnal by the addition of the orange berries.

■ Choose a long, funny-shaped pumpkin, decide which side will be the front and stand it on its stemmed side so that the top is rounded. Then slice off a piece from the back, and scoop out the inside.

■ Cut out whatever shape face you want. It is best to use a small sharp knife for this and to cut out the pumpkin in small pieces rather than trying to cut out, say, the whole mouth as one long slice. Put the night light or candle inside the pumpkin and secure the back on again with a few wires made into the shape of hairpins.

■ Take the two oranges, and cut off a small slice of skin (without reaching the flesh) to make them flat at one end, so that they stand up. With a sharp pointed knife, cut out a hole in the top of the oranges, and scoop out enough of the orange flesh so that you can fit in a small amount of wet florist's foam. Have the florist's foam come out of the orange by at least 2.5 cm (1 in).

■ Insert a candle in the middle of the florist's foam (you can either secure it with wires or buy a candle holder to go into florist's foam from a flower shop).

■ Arrange flowers around the candle, trimming the stems very short and inserting them into the florist's foam at an angle. Allow strands of the foliage to trail around the fruit and dot about the brightly coloured flowers fairly evenly – but not rigidly organised – around the arrangement.

YOU WILL NEED:

Pumpkin
Night light
Oranges
Florist's foam
Anemones (blue)
Berries (orange)
Foliage
Candles

Oranges with their bottoms sliced off make perfect containers for small arrangements built up around a candle. The colour is also most attractive with candle light.

SPECIAL OCCASIONS

91

SPECIAL OCCASIONS

Festive fireplace

What looks like a garland on this mantelpiece is really a group of four trays filled with wet florist's foam that is then covered with masses of flowers and foliage. Unlike a garland that takes a long time to make and then does not last (as the flowers are not in water), flowers arranged in florist's foam should last through the festive season. It is essential, though, that you keep the foam topped up with water and replace any odd flower that dies. This system is also so much easier and quicker to put together.

Depending on the length of the fireplace, fill two to four trays with wet florist's foam. Then, in the centre of the arrangement, secure one to three church candles in place by taping wires, in the shape of hair pins, on to the base of the candles. Then insert them in the florist's foam.

Add the flowers and foliage around the candles and through the whole arrangement. Make sure to position the flowers and foliage so that they flow freely outwards from the centre candles. Also give the garland some shape, tapering the arrangement at the ends of the mantelpiece and allowing the more trailing pieces of greenery to flow down the front.

Trailing ivy and pieces of blue pine interspersed with white and lime green flower heads make the perfect mantelpiece garland for Christmas.

YOU WILL NEED:
2-4 trays
Florist's foam
1-3 church candles
Wire
Lilies (white)
Lilac (white)
Viburnum opulus
Ivy
Variegated pittosporum
Blue pine

SPECIAL OCCASIONS

Cake decoration

Flowers needn't be limited to containers standing on surfaces. Here is a very simple way to make a very effective cake decoration, using leaves and a small group of flowers. Choose flowers that match the cake. Mirroring the richness of the chocolate, deep red roses have been chosen in this design, accompanied by dark green leaves, blackberries and a few white flowers to lighten it.

To make the arrangement, pick 3-4 large ivy leaves, and clean them thoroughly. Then cut a small piece of wet florist's foam (no more than 5 cm [2 in] square at the most), and lay the leaves beneath it. Secure the leaves to the foam by making a couple of hairpin shapes out of pieces of wire (see page 9), and pushing them up through the leaves to the florist's foam. Once this is done, simply insert the flowers and foliage all over the foam. Since the blackberries are so soft, they can simply be placed on the arrangement without securing, or loosely pin them in place with a wire.

The beauty of this way of decorating a cake is that, when the cake is to be cut, the whole arrangement of flowers can be removed. Place it to one side on a small plate, and then neither the cake nor the decor will be damaged. It can remain on the plate throughout the party, as a separate piece of decoration – and will last well, as it is all in wet florist's foam.

YOU WILL NEED:

Florist's foam
Dark green ivy leaves
Smaller trailing ivy
Dark red roses ('Black Magic')
Chincherinchee arabicum
Blackberries

A neat finishing touch for this bedecked cake, is the trail of ivy wound around its base – it has been carefully washed first, of course.

SPECIAL OCCASIONS

Crystal ice bowl

Here is a lovely fresh idea for serving ice cream at a dinner party. You can match the colour and flavour of the ice cream or sorbet with flowers, berries and fruit in the bowl. To make the ice bowl you will need two plastic or glass bowls of sufficiently different size that one will fit inside the other with at least a 5 cm (2 in) gap between them all around. Get plenty of ice cubes ready from their containers and lots of small flowers/berries/petals/leaves of your choice.

- Place a layer of ice at the bottom of the larger bowl, and place the flowers and other items that you are decorating the bowl with between the cubes.

- Stand the smaller bowl on top of this layer and in the centre. Its rim must be at the same level as the rim of the outside bowl and an equal space left between the two bowls all around the edge.

- From there, work your way around the space between the bowls, filling with ice, berries, flowers, leaves, and then more ice, and so on, until you reach the top. Once you have filled up the the gap between the bowls, you will need to put water in it, to fill the spaces between the ice cubes. Before doing so, however, place something flat (a chopping board, for example) on top of the two bowls, as the water can make the smaller bowl float and the whole arrangement will be spoilt. Don't put water in the small bowl.

- Once the water has been poured in, place the bowls in a flat place in the freezer. Leave it there for 24 hours, so that you are sure that the ice is completely solid.

- Take it out of the freezer, and place the bowls under the hot water tap for just enough time to soften the top layer of ice and be able to remove both bowls. You now have a most beautiful bowl made of ice, that looks like crystal. Keep it in the freezer until it is to be used, but it will take at least another day to thaw.

These bowls work best with just a few small flowers – most of the bowl should be simply ice. Large flower heads and fruit detract from the bowl's delicacy.

YOU WILL NEED:

2 plastic or glass bowls of different sizes
Ice cubes
Rose petals (orange)
Hypericum berries
Euphorbia blossom (orange)
Solidago
Small ivy leaves

SPECIAL OCCASIONS

Canapé serving trays

The trouble with canapé serving trays is that once some of the food has been eaten, they begin to look rather bare and uninviting. So, here are two very different ways to dress up trays using fresh flowers to keep them looking delectable. The first tray is made from wicker and the second is a converted old, shallow, market fruit box. Wicker can be difficult to clean, so place squares of clear cellophane on the wicker and under the food, which you can then change when putting on fresh food.

■ For the wicker tray, collect the flowers and foliage you will be using, and make many small bunches with stems that are no longer than 12.5 cm (5 in). Tie them up with raffia or string, leaving the strands long. To achieve a blowsy, pre-Raphaelite look, make the bunches very full and group them together tightly – otherwise it can all end up looking rather coy.

■ Tie the bunches onto the wicker tray, criss-crossing them over each other so that they are facing both ways. Work around only one or two sides of the tray, as covering the tray altogether can hide the food.

■ If you have an old, shallow, market fruit box, have a piece of glass cut to the inside measurements of the tray, and tap in small nails along the inside of the box 2.5 cm (1 in) down from the top. The glass will actually sit on the nails and the food can then rest on the top.

■ Under the glass, fill the box with leaves, petals, roses ... anything you like. Alternatively, consider putting in fruit, tidy rows of vegetables, sea shells, or whatever you feel goes with the food you are serving.

Here are two simple ways of dressing up unusual serving trays for a drinks party.

YOU WILL NEED:
Wicker tray or market fruit box
For the wicker tray:
Raffia or string
Small red open roses ('Vicky Brown')
Rose petals (orange)
Leaves
Berries

For the market fruit box:
Brown roses (Leonidas)
Hypericum berries
Berried ivy
Foliage

Seasonal colour directory

The main flowers in this directory are listed by colour, under their true season. However, flowers are increasingly being imported from other countries, so that we have ended up having tulips in the summer and lily of the valley in the autumn! The importing of flowers has not been taken into account here, but it is worth remembering.

What is also true is that many flowers flow into two or three seasons. Tulips, for example, are spring flowers, but we start seeing them in the shops before Christmas, and have them all the way through to early summer.

On the question of colour, many flowers (such as alstroemeria) are two-tone, so the main colour has been taken as their description.

WHITE/CREAM

Spring:

Allium, arum lily, brodeaia, chincherinchee, convallaria (lily of the valley), ginesta, hyancinth, ixia, lilac, muscari (grape hyacinth), narcissi, ranunculus, scilla, tulip.

Summer:

Achillea (yarrow), alchemilla (lady's mantle), allium, antirhinum (snapdragon), astilbe, astrantia, bouvardia, brodeaia, campanula, dahlia, delphinium, digitalis (foxglove), dill (anethum), godetia, gypsophila, hydrangea, iberis (candytuft), Iceland poppy, liatris, lisianthus (eustoma), lupin, lysimachia, nerine, peony, phlox, scabius, stephanotis, stock, sweet pea, sweet william, tuberose.

Autumn:

Amaryllis, erica (heather), *Euphorbia fulgens*, *E. marginata*.

Winter:

Camaelaucium (wax flower), helleborus (Christmas rose).

All year:

Alstroemeria, antirhinum (snapdragon), aster (September flower), carnation, chrysanthemum, eucaris, freesia, gerbera, gladioli, gypsophila, iris, lily, orchid, protea, rose, trachelium.

SEASONAL COLOUR DIRECTORY

BLUE/PURPLE

Spring:
Anemone, hyacinth, lilac, scilla, tulip.

Summer:
Aconitum (monkshood), agapanthus, ageratum, allium, brodeia, campanula, cornflower, delphinium, echinops, eryngium, gomphrena, hydrangea, lavender, lisianthus (eustoma), lupin, nigella, phlox, scabius, statice, stock, sweet pea, tricytrism, veronica.

Autumn:
Aconitum.

Winter:
Anemone, hyacinth.

All Year:
Alstroemeria, aster (September flower), carnation, chrysanthemum, freesia, gladioli, iris, liatris, orchid, trachelium.

YELLOW

Spring:
Forsythia, genista (broom), grevillea, narcissi, ranunculus, tulip.

Summer:
Achillea (yarrow), allium, antirhinum (snapdragon), calendula (marigold), celosia, cirsium, dahlia, eremerus (foxtail lily), helenium, helianthus (sunflower), Iceland poppy, kniphofia (red hot poker lily), lupin, rudbekia, solidaster, statice, stock.

Autumn:
Euphorbia fulgens, mimosa, zantedeschia.

Winter:
Daffodil, fritillaria, tulip.

All Year:
Alstromeria, carnation, anigozanthus (kangaroo paw), chrysanthemum, freesia, gerbera, gladioli, heliconia, iris, lily, orchid, rose, solidago.

101

SEASONAL COLOUR DIRECTORY

GREEN

Spring:
Moluccella.

Summer:
Dahlia, eucomis (pineapple lily), fennel flower (yellow dill), lupin, sedum.

Autumn:
Amaranthus, chrysamthemum 'Shamrock', hydrangea.

Winter:
Bupleurum, chrysanthemum 'Shamrock', euphorbia.

All Year:
Anigozanthus (kangaroo paw), anthurium, orchid, rose ('Limona').

BURGUNDY/RED

Spring:
Anemone, ixia, ranunculus, tulip.

Summer:
Antirhinum (snapdragon), astilbe, bouvardia, celosia, dahlia, godetia, gomphrena, hydrangea, Iceland poppy, kniphofia (red hot poker lily), lupin, peony, stock, sweet pea, sweet william.

Autumn:
Amaranthus, *Euphorbia fulgens*, antedeschia.

Winter:
Amaryllis.

All year:
Alstroemeria, anigozanthus (kangaroo paw), anthurium, gerbera, ginger lily, gladioli, gloriosa, heliconia, leucadendron 'Safari', protea, rose.

SEASONAL COLOUR DIRECTORY

PINK

Spring:
Anemone, hyacinth, ixia, prunus (peach blossom), ranunculus, tulip.

Summer:
Aster, achillea (yarrow), antirhinum (snapdragon), astilbe, campanula (Canterbury bell), bouvardia, cornflower, chelone, dahlia, delphinium, digitalis (foxglove), godetia, gypsophila, hydrangea, Iceland poppy, lisianthus (eustoma), lupin, nerine, peony, phlox, physostegia, stock, sweet pea, sweet william, zinnia.

Autumn:
Amaryllis, heather (erica), zantedeschia.

Winter:
Camaelaucium (waxflower).

All year:
Alstroemeria, anthurium, carnation, chrysanthemum, freesia, gerbera, ginger lily, gladioli, heliconia, lily, orchid, protea, rose.

ORANGE/PEACH

Spring:
Clivia, ranunculus, tulip.

Summer:
Asclepia, calendula (marigold), carthamus, celosia, crocosmia (montbretia), dahlia, fritillaria (crown imperial lily), godetia, helianthus (sunflower), Iceland poppy, kniphofia (red hot poker lily), stock, sweet pea.

Autumn:
Amaryllis, eremerus (foxtail lily), *Euphorbia fulgens*.

Winter:
Amaryllis, tulip.

All year:
Alstroemeria, carnation, freesia, gerbera, gladioli, heliconia, lily, protea, rose, strelitzia (bird of paradise).

Index

agapanthus, 34
alchemilla, 38
Amaryllis in a long Tom pot, 54
amaryllis plants, 22
anemones, 62, 76, 90
Autumn rust, 60

Basic techniques, 8-9
bear grass, 80
Be-decked tool box, 56
Blue and purple jugs, 34
blue pine, 92
Blues and whites, 16
Burgundy and orange bouquet, 50
butterfly leaves, 80
buying flowers, 8

Cake decoration, 94
camomile (matricaria), 78
Canapé serving trays, 98
Candle centrepiece, 40
cementing in pots, 9
ceramic containers, 15, 29, 35, 71, 77
Chincherinchee arabicum, 94
choisia, 52
Christmas wreath, 86
Citrus fruits and flowers, 44
containers, 9
cornflowers, 38
cotinus leaves, 50, 52, 60
Crystal ice bowl, 96

daffodil plants, 18
Daffodil twig basket, 18
daffodils, 12
delphiniums, 34

eucalyptus, 72
euonymus, variegated, 58
euphorbia, 52
  blossom, 96

Festive fireplace, 92
florist's foam, using, 8
flowers, keeping fresh, 8
  buying, 8
freesias, 32
fruit, in arrangements, 45, 49, 57, 59, 63,
  91, 95

galax leaves, 38, 56
gaultiera leaves, 44, 70, 74
grape hyacinths, see muscari

Halloween pumpkin, 90
Harvest time, 62
hebe leaves, 74
huckleberry foliage, 60
hyacinth plants, 20
hyacinths, 16, 28
hydrangeas, 40, 88
hypericum berries, 60, 96, 98

ivy, 22, 42, 62, 66, 72, 92, 94, 96
ivy berries, 60
ivy, variegated, 60, 74
ivy, with berries, 98

Leafy vases, 80
Leafy wrapping paper, 88
Lemons and sunflowers, 32
leonidas roses, 60
lilac, 92
lilies, 70, 92
Lisianthus wreath, 36

matricaria, 38, 40, 78, 88
Metallic shades, 66
Mexican orange bush, 34
Mixed spring plants, 20
moluccella, 28
monstera leaves, 80
moss, using, 9
muscari (grape hyacinths), 16, 26
muascari (grape hyacinth) plants, 20

napkin rings, 39, 41
narcissi plants, 18, 20
narcissi, 12, 26

Oranges and lemons, 58
Orchids and willow, 68

palm leaves, 80
pansies, 40
parrot tulips, 14
Pastel pots and roses, 42
phalaenopsis orchids, 68
Pink, cream and green, 28
pittosporum, 28
  variegated, 38, 44, 72, 92
Polianthus cups, 14
polianthus plants, 14
pompeii lilies, 70
posies, 27, 51, 95
Primary shades, 76
primulas, 40
protea, 60
  heads, 62, 72

raffia, buying, 9
ranunculus, 26, 44
rhododendron foliage, 56
roses, 32, 38, 42, 44, 50, 52, 60, 62,
  66, 72, 74, 84, 86, 88, 94, 98
  petals, 96, 98
  small, 48
rudbekia, 60
ruscus, 58

scabius, 38
Silver candelabra, 74
solidago, 38, 96
Spring posy, 26
Stone-filled vase, 72
sunflowers, 32
Symmetrical fireplace, 78

terracotta pots, 25, 39, 43, 45, 49, 55,
  63, 79
The dinner table, 48
tin and metal containers, 23, 61, 67, 69
Tin pot amaryllis, 22
Topiary trees, 12
tortured willow, 68
Tree and napkin ring, 38
tropical leaves, 88
tulip plants, 20, 24
tulips, 16, 26, 28, 56, 76
  parrot, 14, 60
Tulips and bamboo, 24
twig basket, 19

Valentine's heart, 84
vases, glass, 13, 17, 33, 53, 73, 81
Vegetable vase, 52
vegetables, in arrangements, 53, 57, 63
Viburnum opulus (guelder rose), 34, 44,
  88, 92
  berries, 72

wax flowers, 28, 56
White simplicity, 70
wires, using, 9
wreaths and garlands, 37, 59, 85, 87, 93

ACKNOWLEDGEMENTS

All the projects in this book were created
by Mary Jane Vaughan except for the
arrangements on pages 6-7 and 29
which were created by Carolyn Bailey;
pages 12, 14, 16, 26 and 34 by Jane
Packer; pages 22 and 24 by The Flower
Van; and page 18 by Steve Woodhams.